14 THROUGH 24

MIKE MAZZILLI

A POETRY ANTHOLOGY

PREFACE

This collection contains over a decade of scattered thoughts; thoughts gained from growing up tumultuously, as most do. Conceived by first loves, heartbreak, grief, failure, and most of all, feeling lost- A work inspired completely by self-doubt, foolish aspiration, fixation, and a certain form of misplaced vanity.

Starting with the poems I wrote at age 14 (the year I discovered writing poetry) and taking us right through the end of adolescence a decade later, this anthology is a journey in the form of journal. It is a timeline of creativity, loosely captured through life-altering events, and all those little defining moments that lie between them. As a side effect of the very nature of youth, there is no solidified thematic through-line in this book other than my own personal chronology and the poetry stemmed from my distinctive reactions and unusual pattern of growth.

In the 9 months it took me to find and assemble these unreleased relics of my past, I've had to relive the memories I've spent much of my life trying to forget. The harsh reaction of which, turned me off to the idea of even finishing this compilation. I wound up putting it off for another year, but after recently turning 25 (the millennial 18), the existential dread of indefinite adulthood settled in, and I decided to make this project a priority. Partly, to feel the encumbrance of the time spent on these writings lifted from me- but partly, to tell a certain truth:

Young/beginner creatives are usually taught to hide their work until it's good by the standards of others. Till they're no longer an embarrassment to themselves and their patrons. These skewed ideals lead artists to become discouraged before they've even had the chance to see the great work they could one day produce, usually killing that creative drive that once burned in them. I am no different. That fear of critique combined with my own unrealistic expectations and perfectionism has made me give up on myself on multiple occasions, causing this internal struggle between my need for an external expression through words, and that gnawing feeling of pointlessness that can nosedive one straight into apathy. When I sank into that darkness, it would take everything I had to become re-motivated. I lost years to these bouts of self-deprecation and dispassion. So the goal here is transparency; to welcome the inadequate along with the eloquent, the ennui with the enthralling, the mediocre with the remarkable- all in a journey of self-acceptance for a self-hypercritical generation.

This anthology is dedicated to every artist who gave up before reaching their full potential. I hope you remind yourself of your passion, as I had to, and that you find charm in the immense imperfections of your work. I hope to read your book, hear your song, see your art, or be impacted in some way by whatever it is you choose to do with the rest of your life- And I hope you have a good time doing it.

CONTENTS

14

Ghost

I am a Ghost beneath this sheet

Below, I can't be heard or seen

But light bleeds through, not too discrete

Linen this thin can't muffle scream

Too thin, just like my mother was

Gave way to fist, not near enough

No pain like that which will become

When love is used to fight with love.

Oh How I Wish

Oh how I wish it wasn't true

Of what I see when I see you

The butterflies, the ocean blue

The stars in sky all midnight through

Skin pillow soft, porcelain smooth

Your hip holds beauty mark tattoo

Like God stole Rembrandt's brush and drew

I look to you, my perfect view

I kiss your lips, I cannot move

Like yours secrete the morning dew

With hair like vinyl record groove

My fingers needles moving through

You're the conundrum I confuse

Your sad song makes it better, Jude

We can't pretend, let's end the ruse

I'll leave, but will come back, my muse.

Oh how I wish it wasn't true

Of what I feel when I feel you.

Soil's Greed

Burnt flowers wither to their knees

They look up to the Sun and beg him, 'Please,

We'd be grateful if you'd hold the heat

We're dying due to soil's greed,

For he doesn't worry of our needs

He used to care about our leaves

As petals wither, he secedes

To save the water which he bleeds,

But we're too weak with disbelief

Too frail to find our own relief

I do not mind all the sorrow and grief

I simply wish to breathe'.

Mellow Drama

Does the drama make you feel

Like a dolphin in a net?

Like there's so much beauty in this world

And you're trapped to feel upset,

But damn, your eyes are gorgeous

So there's just no need to fret,

The remedy for spectacle

Is simply to forget,

If forgetting's not an option

Well here's your other choice,

Go speak love of another-

Don't forget to raise your voice,

And soon, you will find joy again

That net will set you free,

But if distaste makes its way back

Well then, just think of me,

Think of how I need you.

How these words will kill me if kept in,

How I feed off of your love

But you give your energy to them,

We have the chance to heal now

If we drown the rumors while they swim,

Don't let their envy of your love

Make hatred where the love has been.

Presence

The trees here all hang lower

than they ever have before,

You've given me the height I need

but I will always beg for more,

Still I'll walk home and touch every

stop sign along the way,

Remember when I couldn't feel

a thing within my reach today?

And sometimes, when I'm reading

I'll doze off with my glasses on,

But when I do, I wake to find

those words upon the pages gone

And I cannot see through the smudge

so I just fly among the cloud,

Maybe soon I will run into you

but for now, I hope you're proud,

And so, I lie down every night

and listen to your favorite song,

I thought it'd make things better

but I've never been so wrong,

I wish I could use some payphone

that hasn't worked in years,

So I could hear your voice again

without you tracing me to here,

It's obvious you're gone now

still, I'll search and never find you.

But I can't stop. If your conscience

clears, I'll be there to remind you.

Shear

I feel so damn ripped-off

My callused hands begin to bleed,

As I lie on this busy street

Nobody dares to look at me,

I have what everybody wants

But none will ever see,

I'm sorry, I just can't give you

The only thing you want from me,

I'm just too sick of blowing whistles

The hustle/bustle of fiscal year,

I will not make it home to cry

My eyes have shed their final tear,

So grab your handy scissors

And start to shape the sheep you shear,

You Herdsman can take all you need

Because my people feel no fear.

Home

When I was 8, I ran away

from home, $12 in my hand.

I cuddled with the blistering cold,

but dreamt I lied in sand.

I stole my father's jacket, it was big

and black and brooding.

And when I came back, each scream and slap

was somehow only soothing.

15

Borrowed

A tree here today

Is gone tomorrow,

The rain's dried up

The bone is hollow,

A drought of dreams

A stream of sorrow,

My advice to you

I hope you'll follow,

Regret all regrets

With pride to swallow,

And live it up now,

Your time is borrowed.

Stripe

A single stripe

Covers my clothes,

Some flashing light

Bright sky of woes,

Lapse of a night

Kills moon, in throes,

For years, upright

I fight for foes,

And without gripe

My garnish grows,

Shine on, my stripe

For she foreknows.

Rapture

If the world shrinks daily by an inch

Soon we'll all be in a pinch.

Held together, arm to arm,

As above us

Locusts swarm,

The Stars have scars like Van Gogh's ear,

Or lack there of, the constant fear

That we won't make it out alive,

And life above

Won't share the sky.

Perfection

From insignificant freckle to slightest twitch of nose

You are Perfection, for I see you with adjudging eyes

With fiery heart and belly butterflied

You are without flaw

Not character, nor aesthetic

You are a magnet whose attraction lures not only me

Every man whose wishful eyes meet that of your

      immeasurable flesh

Are endlessly drawn

Pound for Pound.

With you, there is no alternation between days of bliss

And those of hell

You are perfection in no sense of the word, because

Words are never perfect

You are perfection in every way I can imagine

And as you can imagine, that breadth breeds wide

      All that matters is I how I see you in my mind.

Cheap Death and Cheat Smile

As we sit and dwell

On spoken things

We fly to hell

On broken wings,

And I kill and lie

So you can care less

About those who die

For your excess.

So move over, move over

You worthless soldier.

You're nothing in this life of mine

If all you hold is lifeless time

Go back to the days, the days you shined

If only you could just rewind

Maybe, just maybe, you might find

That one little reason or rhyme

As to why you feel the way you do inside,

Or the reason you think on the drop of a dime

That it would be better just to die.

So fake that death

You wish to have

And save your breath

You're cold, unclad.

But smile at me

If we pass on the street,

'Cause I need you alive

Though you're my foe

To cover this lie.

No one can know,

The years of pain

You & I have caused

Washed away by the rain

And the deadly pause,

That kills me when I see myself,

Because nobody wants to help.

And that, I fear, is the death of us all.

Because when it comes time to fall

We'll turn our backs on one another

Though we're dying right next to each other.

So fake fearlessness

To please yourself.

And through tactlessness,

Welcome to hell.

Fifty Wise

Keep them close, both tail and eyes

Watch with intent, the fireflies

They'll illuminate the blackened skies

And bring their God to his demise,

All together, Fifty Wise

Congregate between her thighs

Shaken up, but yes alive

Even so, she'll never rise,

Through coroner, and silent sighs

Watch closely now, they're in disguise

I don't mean Gods or Fireflies

I mean, of course, the Fifty Wise.

For they come not from here nor there

One single life, they'd never spare,

And if they come, you best not stare

Don't listen, and move not a hair

For if a life, they know is there

You will be dead without a care,

They rule the night with viselike grasp
Seep into you like poison gas
Each breath will feel like life's last gasp
Won't stop till they complete their task,

And they've come back for just one reason
To kill all those guilty of treason
Descendants of the nonbelievers
Those who killed the nightmare weavers,

A group, a troupe, blasphemy seekers
Beaten, bloody, bound to reapers
They now are the sorrow keepers
Who feed on all, for all are weaker,

They've come for vengeance, your demise
I mean, of course, the Fifty Wise.

They started off as Forty-Five
All put on their knees and slain
But soon, a few five more
Would join them in the pain,

A King, a Queen, a Pastor, Prince

And the Prince's love he'd lain

Terror tamed the guillotine

Even the Princess came

They all kept their flawless count

For it was a Headman's game

No one thought about it for a year

Till they rose again with different name

They showed up late one August night

When the skies refused to rain

Nobody in the whole damned town

Foresaw the coming pain,

Now, those Five were back

Plus Forty Five more

They crept into sleeping house

By slipping through the door

They raped every woman

Left them near dead on the floor

They were bleeding everywhere

Every virgin, every whore,

The men, they could not help

They would just tremble and stare

Their wives and daughters ravaged

Now unable to bear

When all women were motionless

Well, next came the men

They didn't let them plead

They just stole the life from them,

Mothers cried for years when woken

Seeing sons and husbands dead

The daughters all went blind

And most never walked again,

Those women shivered through the night

Even when it wasn't cold

And although almost all survived

They couldn't procreate alone,

Forty years, the women died

That town forever gone

The Fifty Wise were satisfied

In repose, for years withdrawn,

But now they're hungry once again

So they're coming back for more

Don't waste your time trying to hide

Just open up your door

Say goodbye to all the men

And lie down on the floor

Do not think of the pain to come

Or nightmare to ignore,

Just pray for the better days

You did not appreciate before

Wait. What is that I hear?

They're slipping through the doors,

Do not look them in the eyes

Just try to think of blackened skies

Believe in all your Father's lies

And I promise you, you will survive

When they congregate between your thighs

Watch closely now, they're in disguise

But they aren't Gods or fireflies

Here they come,

The Fifty Wise.

16

Today

I may not be able to dance my hands along piano keys,

But I know more songs than I could ever sing.

Each time I sit at that bench I ask myself,

"What shall these fingers play today?"

Every time I look at that painting on the whitewashed wall,

"What does it mean?" I ask. That reflection never answers.

Every morning I look up to the Sun and ask him,

"Which rays will you shine upon my skin today?"

Every morning he looks down on me and replies,

"Whichever ones remind you you're lucky to be alive".

A Smile for The End

My dear, oh my dear

How do you sleep?

I'm wide awake here

My eyes, they weep.

Places we could go

Time we could spend

Brings joy, but I know

One day it'll end.

So tell me those lies

And see me smile

The truth in your eyes?

My last denial.

I won't live without you

So you'll never leave

'Cause you'll have me, too,

And there's nothing we'll need.

Forever Seamed

I did what I could to hold you over

With little quotes and poems

It's been twenty months come October

Time for me to come back home,

And it killed me all those nights

That you didn't write me back

So I hope when I see you tonight,

You'll say the things I need and lack,

I only hope for my own sake

That you didn't deceive me

Maybe the morning of my wake

You'll wish you didn't leave me,

You've got a thousand reasons *"why"*

That I will never understand

Guess patience wasn't worth the time

I'll end this just because you can't,

Your actions are the reasons

For my self-doubt and distress

Was it worth it to please him?

I hope you don't think I'm obsessed,

The last time that I checked it

Passion can be hatred, too

A mutually malignant method

Designed by times I've despised you,

And all you've done was knock me down

You never helped me get back up

Wait, what'd you say just now?

"I'm saying that I'm still in love,

And I know things have changed this year

Over time, we've lost and dreamed

But I can never let you go, I fear

In me, you are forever seamed."

supposed to feel

Is this how a door feels

Every time it gets slammed shut?

Is this how a child feels

From every scrape and cut?

Is this how an old man feels

When he falls and can't get up?

Is this how a woman feels

When she loses everything at once?

Because this is how it feels to me

Getting stabbed in the heart, repeatedly

Like I've lost my friends and family

And I've lost all the good left in me,

Like I've buried my leftover sanity

Gave away my remaining integrity

'Cause my Seeing Eye dog was as blind as me

I'm a Runaway now, that won't stop to bleed,

And this is why, inside I scream

'Cause it hurts like hell, know what I mean?

And I know you do, I KNOW you do

Because, well, you're a human, too,

And we all feel pain all the same

Starts in the heart and instills shame

Sneaks in your soul, leaving it stained

It steals your love till you're but drained,

It becomes your deeper meaning

Engulfs you, like the air you're breathing

It starves you- mother birds when feeding

Deceives you like the words you're reading,

Like the man without hands

Who holds only what he knows

Just like that pauper Devil

Who sold himself his own damned soul,

Like a sorry psycho killer

Who can only kill himself

Like the prince who lost his power

But in the interim gained his wealth,

I sat in the heat of the hate so long

My skin started to peel

I listened to the words of that song

So many times, reality became unreal,

I fear that all I have left to my name

Is what I have yet to steal

So tell me, am I truly insane

Or is this how love is supposed to feel?

As Does It

A poet's palm is pricey

And yet, it still does sweat

Like the king who loses everything

Besides his old regret

Just like my long lost lover

Whom I have never met

Inevitably, the gambler in me

Will have to pay the debt.

And as I do, the rivers flow

As do they, trees sway and grow

And as they do, our vigor slows

But why does it? Nobody knows

That seems to be just how it goes

For normalcy will break all molds,

Sometimes, the best bet is the fold

Sometimes, we're worthless, gilded gold,

But wise words will outweigh the scold

For fortune hates the Brave & Bold

Just listen up, do what you're told

And as you do, young men grow old.

As do they, each day

We'll live a little less and less

And as you do, you will become

Fixated on your own success,

Until the time attacks you back

And you fetishize lack of excess

And as those incongruent thoughts

Put you to their poisoned test,

A baby bluebird leaves its Mother's nest

And flies 400 miles west

And his elders, they are all impressed

But the sorrow drowns what feels the best,

And though he knows he has been blessed

He feels like an unwanted guest

With his own thought, he becomes obsessed

Until his sadness hits its crest,

Putting years of growing up at rest

And so, with death, he was abreast

With the possessed, he pressed and pressed

Till he fell fast, who would've guessed?

He dove, but spoke clear to the nest

His last words said with puffed-out chest

"Tell mama not to hold duress,

I've earned this end. I have transgressed."

It Seems

It seems I've become what I wanted to be

In this beautiful place, all I want is to leave

I have people to love, but none who love me

The friends here aren't the friends that I need,

And it would seem this misery

Has been my one true friend of late

But I hate that he knows everything

About me that I hate,

It seems ocean's what brought me here

To live without purpose, live without fear

For years and years, for me, they'd cheer

Now all I want is this silence to clear,

I've worn out my welcome in places I've built

It's warm, but the people can give you the chills

So I've stacked up all these lives of guilt

Gambled love for a penny's worth of thrills,

So I'll sit back as the pain instills

My conscience feels the pain it kills

The voices shriek while sanity spills

No suicide could silence shrills,

My mind is tearing at the seams

Stability is wrung and reamed

My balance shakes on fragile beams

Subconscious stalls the hopes I dreamed,

So I'll cry and cry till I cannot see

Look at the man in the mirror I'll never be

Because my friend, well it would seem

I can't Love long as I Love me.

17

Whoa

Baby, you're a thornless Rose

A diamond among worthless stones

How you're so perfect, no one knows

You've made me lose all self-control

To think this started with a simple "*Hello*"

So much for "Let's just take things slow"

You're a knockout, and I dropped out-cold

Our first kiss was your first deathblow

I'll hold you high and stay below

Next to you, my heartbeat can't plateau

It seems I'm shot by Cupid's Bow

But I love the ache of your arrow

A paragon of perfect pain that grows

Compared to you, "stunning" is just *so-so*

I can make it to you if I can make it home

But I can't leave with nowhere to go

Wish you weren't trapped in that forgotten borough

Or I wasn't trapped in my own sorrow

In my head, I can find the right words, although

When I see your face all I can say is 'Whoa'.

Sun

Enjoy the Sun today,

'Cause tomorrow,

You'll be sulking in your sorrow,

And after tears, the rain will follow,

A flash flood where you used to wallow.

Nonchalantly,

It's mocking,

Over-intently,

You're watching.

And you'll feel nothing,

'Cause your hands are numb,

As you touch the cold window,

Waiting for the Sun.

And if after some days it still won't come

You'll see a new time in life has begun

In Solace where only laments are sung

And you'll see then, that One always equals None,

As you touch the cold window,

Waiting for the Sun.

TYFS

A distance of three thousand mile

Makes all my longing here futile

But I hope you're happy, all the while

'Cause the world deserves to see you smile.

I wish that I could keep you warm

But I can't be there for the storm

From so damn far, it's so damn hard

But loneliness won't leave you scarred.

When winter weather gets you down

Look in your eyes- careful, don't drown

Can't see your face and feel upset

That mirror holds the best sunset.

How you pine for me, I am befuddled

I can't wait to be next to you, cuddled

And I pray we're together come next spring,

Till then-

Thank You For Smiling.

Chase

Last night, my mind was on you. Who else?

I saw you in every single one of my dreams

And I swear I would've killed myself

If it meant just a few more minutes of sleep,

Now every time I close my eyes

Your face isn't far behind

And it's times like these, to my surprise

I wouldn't mind just going blind,

I hope I'm somewhere in your heart

Like you're ever-rooted in mine

We're so many miles apart

And that would give me peace of mind,

I fear, each minute I'm alive

You'll fall in love with anyone

It could happen at any time

So I close my eyes like moon to sun,

And I pray to God for hours

Which always seem to pass like weeks

But it seems my worry has devoured

My sanity, and now, he shrieks,

So I can find him once again

And put him in his rightful place

For now, my home is with madmen

Who once held love, but now, must chase,

And chase, and chase, and chase for days

Just to catch ephemeral glimpses

What they're willing to do leaves me amazed

They come up short and beg for inches,

And they'll all die too young because

Well, they'll never be happy

And I wish I could accept your flaws

Like I wish you couldn't live without me.

You Wanna Know?

You wanna know how you broke my heart?

The way that would shatter everything

I know in an instant,

Where years from now, I'll be home

and I'll still find small shards of it,

The way concrete breaks when it shakes

hands with a jackhammer,

The way teeth freeze and crumble

from overexerted chatter,

You wanna know how it feels to lose you?

The way it feels to be separated from

a free and flawless diamond,

The way it feels to be lost on an

elapsed, abandoned island,

How it feels to lose my writer's block

and then misplace my pen,

How it feels to fall, get up, trip, slip, stand

then fall again,

You wanna know how it felt to be with you?

My heart was always beating hard

like the wings of leaving dove,

Like love was no longer just something

I was only dreaming of,

When you were riding shotgun, so you couldn't

leave, I'd pray to stall,

Like if you took me back right now

this pain would mean nothing at all,

So please do, please do. You know deep down

it's not him, it's me,

You know we're both hell bound now,

'cause it's a sin to set us free,

So I'll take you back, I promise you,

I can forgive and forget,

But maybe it would hurt too much

for you to relive that regret.

But if it won't, hurry up, please,

because I'm dying here *without you.*

49

Sugarcoat The Revolution

Flood the streets, flood the streets

Where Cairo & Mubarak meet

The revolution has begun

The perfect time to strike has come,

Fight with words all from the heart

Rip his whole regime apart

The casualties will not compare

To joy of breathing freedom's air,

So let us trace Tunisia's tracks

So we can have dignity back

Stop your cautions- Stop warning us

'Cause soon we'll be victorious,

The Dictator has been dealt death

His love has no loyalty left

Now America, we're just like you

We've suffered all that you've been through,

Pride rushes through our sand and soot

With Liberty, we've made it, but

We're unruly? How could that be?

Must we pay the price for being free?

Why Am I Awake?

Tick-tock, it's 3 'o clock

I just can't fucking fall asleep

Wish I could take a soothing walk

Too bad my legs are too damn weak,

So I push my brain against the board

And let my thoughts uselessly race

They're running, as if for reward

But there's no finish lines in space,

I focus on the words of mind

But they're scrambled, so I have no clue

When I think there's nothing left to find

Just when I think my thinking's through,

As I think thought ineffectual

I realize why I'm still up

'Cause you said I was less than dull

But with him, you fell in deepest love.

Freedom

You're a constantly growing malignant cyst

Birthed right in the center of my shrinking heart

Now my every thought of you finds its way to "Bitch"

Guess I always make my way back to the start,

It's over, so forget it, now and forever

We've outrun our ephemeral path

Our connection's been broken and severed

So act unfazed with facade and nervous laugh,

And tell me how you'll 'really miss me'

But that you hope I find "true love"

But I won't try, though you're insisting

'Cause I want to be the one You love,

So forgive me if I seem insane

I went off the track I wasn't on

Days go by, they feel the same

I'm a train on rail, my path is drawn,

I'll always be thinking of us

And what we could've been

I think of that weekend of love

Wasting what we had's a sin,

And I know we didn't last that long

But hey, when you know, you know

I went all-in, but I was wrong

'Cause now I've got nothing to show,

And now, you owe me everything

That time I spent on dying dreams

How I once sailed with winded wing

You owe me that old me, free at sea,

Because all my foreseen oceans

Look tremulous, shadowed, and rough

Floating without love is lonesome

Free as can be, but heart in cuff,

It's better to have loved & lost (?)

Even if you were a succubus

And though I'm still paying the cost

Can't help but wish there was an *Us*,

So I'll stay incapacitated

It seems I cannot just "move on"

I'm manacled to you, I hate it

You won't turn key to free a fawn,

These chains that fasten me to you

A truth that brought me bended knees

Still, after all that I've gone through

I'd never pray for my release,

'Cause there is just no chance of freedom

In the end, I'll want to be with you

This thought is one I'll have to fathom:

I only want freedom if I'm free with you.

18

All Irony

Just as the moons wax and wane

One second you're crazy, the next you're insane

But these endless days of progress pain

Are nothing compared to the scars I'll gain.

Hide me from your best of friends

Then flaunt me to your enemies

Love me now, you'll hate me when this ends

When your thresholds meet my boundaries.

I never knew why you played puerile games

Didn't think you were that kind of girl

I loved the way you consistently changed

And I'll miss you so, my charming churl.

I can only remember the good I forgot

Every single time you cross my mind

But correlatively, you're just One Gunshot

I aimed directly at my spine.

Dear Friend

Dear friend,

I was born premature.
You are the incubator that assured my survival,

I learned too fast.
You are the finger that flipped the pages of my book,

I've outgrown my youth.
You are the food that quelled my hunger pangs,

I've lived too heavy.
You are the chariot that rode me directly into the sun,

And now I'm leaving.
But you are here to keep my memory alive,

I'll put in a good word for you, I promise
I love you, my friend. Please, tell them about me.

Rejoice

I'm feeling up

I'm feeling low

Good times, they come

Those comings go.

A wishful pair of lonely eyes

Creates a world in perfect black

The last vein of my heart unties

And all I hold, is holding back.

'Boom, Boom,' thumps my murmured heart

As I draw the shades of hotel room

Right now, my wish is to restart

So let this bed become my tomb.

I've writ a note- my eyes are shut

I lay head back, I pull the trigger

I've ended this untimely rut

So let me rejoice in my Rigor.

Wings

Lying on my back, Widows looking down

Their nails tapping cloud, the strangest of sound

My blood feels rushed, my heart starts to pound

The river slows, then water builds all around

And as if one, all trees stop growing

The winds of color pause their blowing

The sun I knew ceases its glowing

Still all the wise men speak of *knowing*

Failure we'll feel on future nights

That golden gray of dimming lights

Though it's early, end is in my sights

I'll read myself my own last rites

A dying man, fever blazed high

Sees shadowed women, laced up to eye

He's scared for his mother, she doesn't know why

She waits for him saying 'Fly, Son. Fly."

You Never Know

Sometimes, we simply wish to fly

At night, within sinister sky

But this weighted World we always bear

Will hold us out of freedom's air

Our feathers drenched by waters white

Please pardon all the prior plight

Wring out the flood from wetted wings

Sear out the sting that torrent brings

Peer at the pier, a seagull sings

A sloppy shriek, he squawks and springs

Yet, he'll find his joy, even though

He's hungry, clumsy, and quickly slow

He'll stumble down to clear-cut ocean

Find love in sand and friends in motion

So learn from that awfully awkward bird

And copy his grace when you use your word

The swords of term can cruelly curse

Conversation can kill, and so can verse

So swerve intuition and preconception

Help those who are lost find new direction

And listen back for small correction

To save you from your misconception

But it's not your fault, don't blame yourself

Just put your trust in someone else,

Irreversible, may life return

After you're gone, you still can learn

That as above, so is below

Use advantage to advance lost soul

'Cause soon you'll be cold on the side of the road,

And One you helped might help back,

You never know.

Your Smile

I could sit here and talk a while

About the way you look and speak

But I have no words for your smile

The way your lips fall to your teeth

I could talk of your honeyed hair

I could talk of your chocolate eyes

Or the way you live with deepest care

How you make me love what I despise

The way you laugh, the way you cry,

The way you smell, the way you touch-

I can put in words, but I can't lie

I love that smile too damn much

Injustice to It would be sin

And that's why I'll keep my mouth shut

I'd pontificate, but I can't win

Because no words would be enough.

Overtime

I tried to watch the sun come up

For once, I wasn't sure it would

So I took all your evil love

And turned it into something good,

Each night, I lie you down on flowers

And watch the suns set in your eyes

Then I stay awake through darkest hours

So I can watch those two suns rise,

Though I might die from sleepless night

As long as you love me for me

I don't care if I lose that light

Just don't love for what I *could* be,

And I won't mind working overtime

Though the smallest sands slip through the glass

But if you slide through my hands, so fine

Then the time I've given you won't pass.

Fight

I saw the light

And I went blind

Lost without sight

And without mind,

Continued on

This road called life

With my hope gone

I sat in strife,

Sank faster than

Was possible

My master's hand:

Unstoppable,

Her prowess of power

Was felt from afar

She could make you cower

Like dark from a star,

So I sat back

Embraced the pain

Can't escape that

Unnerving reign,

That She had over everyone

She'd forced even upon the gods

For she was strong as any Sun

She mercy murdered all the frauds,

So be careful of what you speak

For She hears all your hollow words

And careful what you choose to think

Because your mind's already Hers,

The only things here that are safe

Are those that don't exist

But I will not lose faceless faith

I'll proceed to resist,

Although She knows

That I can't see

And She controls

Each part of me,

I no longer fear anything

For I have seen the worst

Suffocation by Saturn ring

And death by Her Perfection Curse,

So join me here while you still can

I promise better than it's been

Come grab my hand and fight for them

So all your boys can become men,

We'll fight for how it was back then

For future saint with past of sin

I can promise you a prideful whim

I just won't promise that we'll win.

19

Weight

We carry Weight that grows with us
It makes this life harder to live
Now we would break the branches that
We once hung off as little kids
But our bodies will snap soon, too
Along with dreams we've left in grinds
We used to waken with the sun
Where now we only draw the blinds.

Won't feel alive till we've found love-
Love temporary/dead already.
The more you attempt, the less you get,
She shakes if you try to keep Her steady.

Imperfect Eyes

I look in the mirror. What do I see?

Imperfect eyes stare back at me

With skin deep sin to set me free

Trapped in this lack of harmony

But sadly, I cannot just leave

To humiliate humility,

With no regard for growing size

They come to help with word so wise

"It only matters what's inside"

But we are all food for the flies

Leave me to be without the lies-

I'll stare back at imperfect eyes.

We'll Call It Equal

I slide,

My finger upon your skin.

I'm high,

On the rush of lust within.

I walk my hands around your hills,

And stop your tears like windowsills,

Do catch the fall of Autumn rain,

To snatch away and kill your pain,

Throw it away, though all in vain,

Lust, Love. To you, it's all the same,

A sophomoric game perfectly played

By the more intuitive of us two,

Misconstrued, but not before I'm swayed

Because it's you. It's always you.

So kill me, please.

Leave me for the Carrion Beetles,

I'll still only want you beneath the steeple.

But we're past that now, it's come down to evil,

So I'll kill you back-

We'll call it equal.

I, Thy Savior

I, thy savior, rest tonight

And put food on thy plate,

I'll take hold of all thy evils

I won't let them escape,

I will save thee if I can

If it not be too late,

From what some people hate the most-

Other people's hate,

I might even save thee

From thy misguided fate,

But the only thing I cannot save

Is thee from thy own faith,

Can't save inertia from the trees

Nor the fall of Autumn leaves,

But that, you cannot blame on me

The fault is Newton's gravity,

In lying birds who love to bleed

Those premature that pass their seed,

Women who never learned to leave

Children who never made-believe,

This is so sad, we all agree

But your Savior will savor me,

'Cause I may punish all good deed

If selfish does the goodness be.

Wall

The steeper the mountain,

The faster the fall,

The deeper foundation,

The stronger the wall,

     And you have the deepest foundation of all.

But in time, I pray

I can break you down

And as your rubble lay

'Cross broken ground,

This sequence of secrets

I've built 'round our lives

Will shatter regrets

Memory of our lies,

But you're still up in front of me

How? Guess I will never know

You can't crumble, because of me

We've tangled root and I can't grow,

Now I see you're a part of me

We're stone and tree becoming One

But you've destroyed the heart of me

And we can't crumble into None,

Still, I will climb. And without use

So thought of you can't hold me down

You may have tangled with my roots

But I will soon see all the sound,

For muffled and amazing wave

I can't swim, but I want to be

The only person that you gave

A chance to grow, a chance to leave,

You've kept me from normality

So long, I don't know what that is

Demolishing is fallacy

'Cause your Wall won't come down for shit.

Only Words

Lies, truths,

They're only words,

Inevitable nothings

To get on your nerves,

Old memories, you can't unglue,

With old disdain, you can't undo,

Back for thirds

With bad tattoo,

New cowards,

A course for two,

But here We are,

Just both absurds,

It's all a waste,

They're only words.

Everything

Here I am, I'm everything

But happy for a world in love

There's so much joy we both could bring

But I'm all you've been thinking of,

I am everything to you

You would not survive without me

And I promise to see us through

'Cause you've done everything, but doubt me,

I am everything to myself

And I know I'm alone in laughing

But tell me, who needs endless wealth?

When I'm the only thing worth having,

I am everything to everyone

At least, I thought this way last Fall

But now, I've come to find at once

That really, we're nothing at all.

Balcony

Our love was born above this roof
You made me build the house for proof

That balcony became our fall
I woke up cold near windowed wall

You kissed me warm like morning sun
A steady slow through Summer's sum

A scorching breeze to breathe in love
Diluted by delusions of

Sincerity that lacked constraint
Ashamed by solitary saint

But here now on the hundredth day
In rooms with beds to breed decay

And you, too genuine for doubt
Bled purple onto grounds of drought

In blackest code of consequence
I lied to you, in confidence

That bond we formed from sickness gone
Compared accounts of life withdrawn

This song I scream became your pain
My limelight died by structured vain

My feet failed when the floor fell through
On sunken stage, I sing for you

And I'm still here- forever here
If always only lasts the year

Sunflower sleep, here comes your moon
Goodnight. Goodbye. I'll love you soon.

20

Eradication

Today, I cried like a little bitch

For the first time in fourteen years

The more they fell, the more I wished

That you were there to catch my tears,

But you are long gone, and I'm jealous

You don't have to see what I feel

'Cause now I really know what hell is

And I'll need more than time to heal,

So keep running. Just keep running

All thoughts of me are thoughts in vain

I tried to keep us from becoming

Another symptom of the pain,

Eradicate us, so I can learn

What it's like to have a little closure

Please cut the ropes that friction burn

Me every time you pull me closer,

So that I can escape from you

So I can feel the free you know

Because you've split me into two

And I've lost parts I can't regrow,

Though you said I would ricochet

That I would be completely fine

Now you have turned my white to gray

A seasoned ghost without a spine,

So I will live on purposeless

You were the one that held me back

I traded dreams of happiness

To be a small part of your past,

I feel like death has called my heart

And told it that the end has come

But you won't be found in the dark

And I can't see the light by sun,

You told me that you'll always love me

But you're not "*in love*" anymore

And when you let me go, abruptly

We wished happiness back and forth,

I guess I meant it at the time

But I hoped you'd crawl back to me

Once you had realized I was fine

I'd tell you to stay on your knees,

But I'll let my hope hold me over

And Until then, I must move on

I knew you'd show, soon as I chose her

You thought I'd want you? You were wrong,

The eradication was quite sour

But vindication's bittersweet

I won't miss you, my misted flower

Though you meant everything to me.

3800

I Promised to love you till the day that I die,
Until you've stopped breathing, I will be by your side.

Hold your hand every morning, cry for you every night,
Stroke your hair till you sleep, never leaving my sight.

I'll pray although God has broken this heart,
I'll hemorrhage forgiveness till you have to part.

Our Children must go, they'll come back when they can,
Our branches must grow, they know you'd understand.

Thirty-Eight Hundred days, I sat by your side,
Waiting and loving, till today when you died.

But I'll carry you on till it's my time to pass,
I'll be at your side soon, it can't come too fast.

For your love is my ship, my vessel, my flight,
And I'll ride it as quick as I can toward the light.

Blind

For months now, I've been going blind

But I saw today in prior time

So have my eyes really been fine?

Was the ailment only in my mind?

When they all tell you differently

A trust dies with intent to see

You must listen to yourself and me

Two voices that you'll hear for free,

But recently, I don't believe

In craziness, for Monkey See

Hallucinate, and hate the greed

That you had driven up and teed,

Sometimes, some lies get in the way

Use eyes to hear the truth, they say

All dying cold, just not today

All crying wolf in great dismay,

So to speak, the words of vision

Is beauty but the missing mission?

Stream the conscious, never listen

Stick to move, then change position,

Stuck in love, too far between

No lid to put on, Evergreen

With no blue sea to tie the seam

So much to see and, too, be seen,

But how can I be really sure

That peace is perfect and impure?

Will we become the lying cure?

We will not sink, just rest ashore,

For I can still look at the sky

And ask to see with unlocked eye

'Cause soon, I'll sleep and wake to find

That all along, we've all been blind.

Our End

Well, well, well. Welcome back, my friends

Here forever? Guess that depends

Wonder if this breaks once it bends?

Ponder what's coming when it ends?

Then all my veins come to a still

I'm falling free, against my will

I'm numb from 3rd and final pill

The room spins black and I turn chill,

Then I hit soft carpeted floor

I've never dreamt like this before

I walk around to just explore

I see the past and what's in store,

Above, I see a golden door

Written on it, "Are you sure?"

Inside is only whitewashed lure

And shadowed body on the floor,

It turns, there's pain inside my core

Because I see my love, Lenore

Her beauty forces me to pore

As she stares back with eyes of ore,

She says "Hello, my lovely boor

I've missed you with a love, restored

I wished for this throughout my core

But I can't be with you, I swore,

That I would kill what I adore

And though you'd like to love me more

I am ending our mending war,

So this is our end, mi amor-

This is our end, mi amor."

You Are the Eye

"It's not your fault."- A poor man's words
If money's made by wisdom's wail
No one's to blame for callow hurts
If all first loves were made to fail

Untimely, but you'll never know
How long I would postpone for you
A stillborn love, but still for show
I'd take this bed and burn it blue

I took apart the love you gave
And reassembled it to lust
So with each misery I save
Sincerity becomes mistrust

Because of us, in lapse of sin
You'll overcomplicate the truth
I broke you in from soul to skin
We traded knowledge in for youth

But here now on our dying day
With all disdain and no remorse
I learned from you that love will stray
If lovers keep it straight by force

When quiet comes, keep basking brief
That peace you crave will burn you dry
Let's say goodbye in love's relief
I need the storm- You are the Eye.

21

For the Best

We were never together
We had a child- a mistake
So leave quietly, please
I hate you more when he's awake
I love you, but don't need you
All you gave him was a name
He'll grow old, you'll be gone
and in the end, we'll die the same.

He'll never know what family
feels like- That's for the best
He'll burn out quick and bright
And blaze a trail of his own mess
Nothing to hold him back, but
the first girl to break his heart
He'll be alone in gray, and raise
a child to pass on the scar.

We live this endless cycle-
A circle of lust, love, and regrets
But for our child in the other room,
you should leave-
                    -It's for the best.

27-8

I crossed the crooked overpass

at 4 Ante Meridiem,

I stopped for just a second

floating right above the median,

I had this car crash daydream of

two beasts as they collide,

I could take this highway either

way, I'd just have to decide,

But choices are but choices now-

both difficult, or day-to-day,

So I can stay and free myself

or travel shackled to these chains,

And in the end, it won't quite

matter if I fall or stand,

'Cause in the end, I know

I'll be exactly where I am.

The Day is Born

Cigarette Cellophane

Warm & Wet. Summer rain

All the sweat, all the pain

Give & Get- Lover's stain.

She

She told me I'm a rolling stone
That She knows one day I'll be gone
Right now you see just skin and bone
But She knows one day I'll be strong.

A soldier's soul, for fear and faith
Hands blistered from a naive hope
It's faint, but She still sees my wraith
While clinging to that falling rope.

She loved to give Her love away
But knew it would not be returned
She thought She thrived in disarray
She tried. She failed. She never learned.

I came up cold with mummer's tongue
To Her, I seem to speak in songs
I'd leave, but trust me, She would come
Where I am is where She belongs.

Wisdom Wasted

Your life will flicker quicker than that failing green
      fluorescent bulb

You'll try to put it down in words, you'll just end up
      with paper pulp,

Your love can grow up sicker than a stationed stone
      of musty mold

And hearts will become colder than a drifter's soul
      already sold

And though it won't get easier, the game seems
      simpler when you're old

'Cause after losing once or twice, you'll know exactly
      when to fold,

And folding hands will soon become your only way
      to slightly win

'Cause when the game was rigged to lose, it's best to
      let the sadness in

But on that dying day, when you are withered down
      to waifly trim

You'll know the wisdom you wasted was kindly kin
      to orphaned sin.

I Drift

This is a song of sweet divorce

Of All-American true love

And so, we've let it run its course

In aftermath, we'll float above

Now as she crosses that state line

She carries Crosses through the mud

Got California on her mind

But Carolina in her blood

And as she drives away, I drift

Solemnity, with paramour

I'm but a slowly sinking ship

Dreaming of flame I've held before

But Her beacon is all burnt out
And I fear it's forevermore
After the years, I've chosen now
To cease my searching for the shore

I've been too long afloat; alone
Sick with this hungry thirst, unsure
I'll spend all night at sea- my home
Just praying for a coastline cure

And still, they board in hopeful band
Convinced my love has not been spent
You'll live with ease on balanced land
And be left with your Discontent.

22

One/None

One heart to shift from room to room

That always seemed normal to me

One soul filled with a red balloon

So you can fly away and leave,

One head filled with some sappy song

And years of haunted memory

One pair of eyes to sing along

To words you hoped to never see,

One hand to hold an empty hand

Your other holds an empty glass

One pair of legs so you can stand

On anything, but broken past,

One waist so you won't waste away

The day before she's given up

One little boy who wished you'd stayed

So he never quite learned to love,

One Whiskeyed wife for novelty

With three women to string along

One Baby Grand missing a key

So you can't play your favorite song,

One big blanket to cover up

That face you never could forget

One pill to keep a lover up

'Cause you can't make her leave just yet,

One picture to soak up the bad

That blood you've spilt with no regard

One promise, not so ironclad

To never leave if things got hard,

One ballerina of the snow

Still shattered in a velvet bed

One pillow to soften the blow

But none to rest your weary head.

Visit Soon

The tree that we made love beneath collapsed in last
    night's storm.
A timely metaphor this world gave back to me,

But I've lived under your influence for months.
The white rum on your lips stained mine,

The taste of whiplash in the morning
Was all that I had left of you,

The heartbeat in my head reminded me
Of all the good we could've held,

The poster children, You & I,
For a warm wasted potential

With white sand beneath our feet
All we could speak of was the black cloud above,

Your doubt became a tidal wave
And collided into what should've been,

That high tide turned shy.
When it receded, you washed away willingly,

    Still, I hope you're ok,
Come back and visit soon.

9/8

I am the one you should admire
I've been so sanctified, of late
I'm not a fighter for the fire
Nor a General of the faith,

I am but one stick in the pyre
You're lying in my burning wake
I used to blaze a little higher
I guess the habit didn't take,

My mistake became your cryptic cause
But not so low that you could see
All the light you gleamed upon my flaws
For shadowed, sweet uncertainty,

But we, the Wise don't believe in rhyme
No clever word could kill the beast
If you speak, best shed your metered mime
You'll be well-fed before the feast.

Seneca

Goodnight, my Youngest Love,

we'll all grow closer from your tragedy,

Are promises enough

to turn a white lie into memory?

I'll be Saint Thomas if

you will stay loyal past the blasphemy.

And I'll be honest with

you- The last thing you want is honesty.

Blank

I've got a bomb in a shoe box

A blank note in a black backpack

A best friend with his blue tongue locked

A brother with a broken back

Sold all my love for a dead thrill

I only kept what you don't need

I'd trade a vein for a spine chill

I'd fight with fire for some heat

Not forced to give a 2nd chance

If there is no point to the pen

Don't clench their hand to hold a glance

But write it in blood if you can

Then let me swarm in that sickness

Choke on the milk of your mother

Tear up your bullet-point wishlist

Pray for the loss of your lover.

ensign.

THEY WEREN'T GOLD, STILL COULDN'T STAY

NOTHING TO HOLD, BUT FADING LIGHT

A STORY TOLD, TOO FAR AWAY

'CAUSE THERE WAS NO GOOD FIGHT TO FIGHT,

NO FOLDED FLAGS FOR FOOLISH YOUTH

NO BODYBAGS TO BREAK THE CHAINS

ALL SILENCE GAGS TO SPEAK THE TRUTH

ALL SUNSHINE DRAGS—

—UNTIL IT RAINS.

23

.illiterate.

I gave her love that you deserve

My best is gone, so is that time

All parallel is peaceful curve

You'll pay the price. I'm past my prime,

So sorry for the haste of lust

She's had me in a hundred ways

I've learned control through pure distrust

Through grace of my Throwaway Days,

But you'll stay through the pain of me

-Too illiterate to read you're right-

And you'll think it insane of me

To stay with you, in spite of spite,

Sheltered from your serenity

I'm vertigo by steady wave

I've lost some nights in reverie

And I can't get back what I gave.

The Brave

We're all born free
And die in chain
Slaves to a dream,
Liberty veined.

All built upon the Evergreen
From desert sand to ocean wave
We're all America, the Greed,
All for America: The Brave.

flower.

I remember the first time I heard my Mother

roar tenderly to protect me.

I knew back then,

even the best of men

don't deserve good women.

I can recall when my first Love wept for me.

I told her not to, but she wouldn't stop.

She said I had no right

to tell her how to love,

and she was right.

I was always too lucky without gratitude.

And I'm lucky now to be surrounded by you.

You are a bouquet of only thorns.

Your love stems from the pain and only I can touch-

I promise to appreciate each ache.

(S)WALLOW

A cracked eye reignites the day.
Dawn for Mothers; some to suffer.
There is no universal joy.
Sad for one might save another,

Don't shackle yourself to ideals
Current, 'cause you are bound to change.
It happens quite without consent,
For we cannot predict the strange,

But if you do find comfort, don't
Forget to force-feed happiness.
To you and everyone around,
Until, at last, they've all known bliss,

And if they all choke by your hand,
Just remind them of your favor.
If they never breathe hope again,
You will know the taste I savor.

Somewhere

I felt numbness in that
lack of diegesis.
The story in me turned
into song. slow and steady,
But not strong enough to stand on

I got used to the words in
my head no one else could hear.
But still, I would not
call-or-respond, for that
earworm fear still plagued me

Lately, I've found myself
humming along to silence.
A Whole Rest to upset those
who somehow still love me. A Longa of
longing for lost love and ubiquity

But I am done standing
still, hoping for the noise I need.
I will let my footsteps be the beat
that moves in me.
Soon this trapped melody will spill

And no longer will I
walk this world with a random touch.
For I've learned no road is truly
better traveled, but that I must
just continue to walk-

And I'll end up Somewhere with a song.

Gold

I doubt the things I used to trust

The Gold I held has turned to rust

So I will lie upon the cusp

Of where I am and who I was,

Now being lost is too routine

We find words to admit defeat

While wild wanderers convene

Right where the crooked crossroads meet,

Assemble. Then we'll disengage

To waste away a storied love

Read empty words to turn a page

We'll find home if we stray enough,

Or just complain to make it right

Complacency to aching sting

You strain yourself to sit all night

But still envy the crown of King,

For this is how we all get burned

Desired dreams we don't deserve

Cannot put faith in what we've learned

If we all shape the bell to curve,

So blend, you monotonic tile

Travel as one until we merge

Line up to fail in single file

If you'd die just to hear a dirge,

Then how could we all be entitled

To laws of all of those distinct

Disown what you discern as wild

Then you'll have time to be succinct,

Salvation's one forfeit away

Accept you won't hold what you crave

And save yourself from Golden Sway

Undying lies, from greed to grave.

24

Alter/Altar

No wrong nor Right in life and death

When opinion is the faith that's Left

Blood lust vs blessed ignorance

Send hounds for scent of common sense,

An altered book will bear no truth

So wise, just like a wisdom tooth

There's pain. We pull, refrain, then shoot

Plant poison in tomorrow's youth,

Give words the meaning that you want

Forge saviors when the world is gaunt

Here, truth isn't all that dire

Kill the truth to praise the liar,

For No Lives Matter when unknown
Can't breathe together? Choke alone
Cutthroat, until we're all but dead
Then be perplexed when you bleed red,

Well peace breed peace, the West is won
We settled for the setting Sun
Practice your preach, sweet Sovereign State
You're Right to overpopulate,

And suddenly, we're holy light
Our scripture sound: The Bill of Rights
May Soldier's ground 'come Veteran soil
War's over now- enjoy the toil.

amber, and her elegy

"Only gold can stay" she said,
as she rolled out my bed
she dipped her tongue in diamond
then kissed me goodbye.
My sheets all stained in silver-
By Purity & Poison.

Her mother's voice echoed through
her throat. "You are not good
enough for me".
I still can hear those words some nights
when alone, or drowning in
company I never tried to keep.
Whether making loveless love
or aching for the hands of her,
that flame I carry almost killed me.
Soaking into pallid skin once too soft for touch.
Her fired feel became my blistered bold-
Through Virtue & Venom.

My days begin and end by
the breath of pyrite now
I took a bite, she did not bend.
Fooled Again.
Just. Like. Yesterday.
I cut my teeth on her and lost my smile.
Letting love leave was the talent attained.
"Only gold can stay" she used to say, and now,
we are gone.

Tritone

I sculpt, you are my model muse
3 Years, I have carved into you
I've whittled words in blood-red hues,
"I wish you saw you as I do."

I preach, you are the phantom prose
Spring has stalled, the chill has risen
Uproot my love before it grows
Keep it in your profit prison,

I forge, you're framed in platinum
With no shame for your elegance
Teach me to breathe in Spanish Sun
Then bury me in innocence,

Composed, and you're the voice I choose
Sing me, but in the key of blue
You bring beauty to my bad news
My tritone, but we still ring true.

Soliloquy. Or a Decade Lost

We slept without intent to wake
No trouble there, what came had passed
But there's this dream I couldn't shake
With you subjected to its vast

We weren't there for common sense
It wasn't just for story's sake
I burned our bridge to mend a fence
And blazed at Green-Eyed glory's stake

For me, the hope was too reposed
I pined for time. I smoldered- yearned
My years of ignorance disclosed
By latency of love returned

Oblivious to dissonance
Forgotten for a freedom found
The sweet of that sufficient bliss
Delayed desire for the sound

A voice I heard when I was young
With words of wisdom, timbre shrill
It spoke of all things soon to come
I shook, but it was soothing still

I shivered till the Winter waned
Dead memory sank to my roots
I waxed away when Summer came
A slave to save the tongue of mutes

I grew strong past the Equinox
Then found a love I knew I'd lose
Though necessary to detox
That Spring that sheltered me in blues

I waded through my chapters blurred
A year of affect, all but failed
I felt the peace within you stirred
We lied inside its coffin, nailed

The silk of night sweat on my skin
Became the Coat of Arms I knew
Too drenched in my drab not to swim
A turn of Archimedes' Screw

"So ramble on," my Father said
As he grew deafer by the day
Wanted my music in his head
But he'd still turn his ear away

So now, I know not what he hears
My Mother says it's all select
If we could practice pain for years
It'd be a talent she'd perfect

We stood upon the fault line crack
We eulogized our childhood
Assembled years in wobbly stack
Then toppled it for our own good

I didn't crumble 'neath the weight
I learned to live in rubbled scorn
But knew with no excuse for hate
That years would fleet as they were born

But we were beaten in the blood
Millenium in saturation
Aligned, we floated through the flood
Stagnant by invalidation

And in that sea of static wave?
Ambiguous morality
We basked in praise to misbehave
Too conscious of mortality

They gave away a slandered name
Was me & me, too free to stand
Forced death on diamond standard shame
Obliged, but to Nostalgia's Hand

I leaned into the retrospect
From shore to shore, the same sublime
I got lost in the disconnect
Then long searched for the absent time

At first we grieved, then secondly
I heaved away the need to crawl
But then, the blue light beckoned me-
I knew I had to heed the call.

25

25 Tonight,
And only 25% of where I thought I'd be by now.
My forward motion is self-delayed, I fear,
by fear.
We spend the riches of youth on dreams
and adulthood learning to let them die.
Is it better to speed & complete,
or to protect the future by postponing it
?
"If we never tried, we never failed."
.derivative.
You can measure longevity,
but not ingenuity-
Not fulfillment.
You can test for intelligence,
but not will,
Nor wisdom.
So I think myself a fool-
And still a failure,
but still at the 1/4 mark.
The stall is my fault.
and it's not.
It's my mother & father's, too.
For I was not a prodigy-
Not, at least, in the things I cared most about.
Any possible potential
was wasted in pure mania,

Maybe passions purposely
lead us down the wrong path.
Maybe some of us are meant to choose wrong
-

But can we change that?
Can the bold beat fate?
If I charge to the end
will I lose my light?
If I choose not to rush
will I still have time?
Is staying true to myself noble
if I die in obscurity?
Will the love of cynics
make this all worthwhile?
Is time spent on love time actually
wasted?
Can we do good and also be great?
Are we predisposed to pointlessness?
Is it ever worth the effort?
Does anything we do even matter?

Yes
No

(Circle One)